Beautifully Embroidered

RACHEL MISERE

Beautifully Embroidered

© 2017 Divine Works Publishing, LLC.

All rights reserved. No part of this publication may be reproduced, stored in a retrieval system or transmitted in any form or by any means, electronic, mechanical, photocopying, recording or otherwise without the prior permission of the publisher or in accordance with the provisions of the Copyright, Designs and Patents Act 1988 or under the terms of any license permitting limited copying issued by the Copyright Licensing Agency.

ISBN-13: 978-0-9996047-1-7

Divine Works Publishing, LLC.
Royal Palm Beach, Florida USA
www.divineworkspublishing.com
561-990-BOOK (2665)

All of the glory belongs

to God

He deserves it!

He is worth the exaltation

He deserves it!

We have been sewn beautifully by Him

We thank Him!

I am loved, You are loved

You are *Beautifully Embroidered*

by God.

Rachel Misere

*God sees you differently
than you see yourself.
You are beautiful
in the eyes of God
Yes, You!*

Dedication:

The words embedded within these pages are full of love, strength, and power and are dedicated to all women who have not felt up to par physically, emotionally, and spiritually. You are precious pearls in the eyes of God, you have been beautifully embroidered by the master potter. Enjoy these words with gladness and confidence in the Lord.

Acknowledgment:

When the Lord assigns you to do something, he always places people in our path to help fulfill that project.

I first thank the Almighty for using me as a vessel for his divine works.

All of the awesome people who took the time to read, listen, pray, and encourage me and those who offered constructive criticism, I thank you from the bottom of my heart.

I am ever so grateful and honored to work with Divine Works Publishing who displayed an immense amount of patience, kindness, and professionalism in bringing this book to fruition.

CHAPTER 1

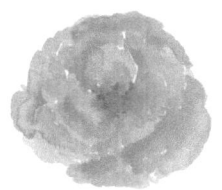

You are Beautifully Embroidered

"I gave you lovely jewelry, bracelets, beautiful necklaces. I gave you expensive clothing of fine linen and silk beautifully embroidered, and sandals made of fine goatskin leather." - Ezekiel 16:10

The definition of embroidery is as such according to Google:

em•broi•der•y
em'broid(ə)rē/
Noun
    1. The art or pastime of embroidering cloth.
    2. Embellishment or exaggeration in the description or reporting of an event. *"Fanciful embroidery of the facts"*
    synonyms: elaboration, embellishment, adornment, ornamentation, coloring, enhancement.

This definition helps to illustrate how you have been finely fashioned and meticulously created by the Lord. The moment you realize that you have been hand-sewn by the Lord is a most beautiful gift. It's a moment of deep realization and deep reflection.

God, then decorates us with talents to be used for his glory. Once we look inward we can see and appreciate our unique gifts and talents. We all have something that is unique and special to offer the world. As we grow in Him, we uncover what these are.

God took his precious time to sew you with intricate parts; every organ in your body is valuable. You are a fine ornament that was polished and embroidered for God's glory because He adores you.

He created you, because he simply loves you. He desires you to be his child; his beautifully embroidered daughter, – so he took time out to create you. Remember, an artist must first have a vision before he creates a masterpiece.

God had a vision. He processed it. Then He took action to bring that vision to fruition. God, your divine master had a vision of you when he created you. He knew all that you would struggle with and where your strengths would be. Every part of you is created for His pleasure and for His glory.

You are beautifully embroidered, perfected by our divine daddy. You do not lack anything nor do you need to add anything to your body which is a masterpiece pottered by God. Cosmetic Surgeries, Tattoos, Piercings, or any other enhancement ... cannot replace his handiwork.

Embrace yourself exactly as you are. Accept your features, your body, your hair, your height, your complexion, everything about you is perfectly and divinely assembled.

Declaration:

I love and accept everything about myself. God will use both my shortcomings and my strengths in great ways.

#Beautifully Embroidered

CHAPTER 2

You are Wonderfully Unique

God doesn't do replicas; you do not have the same DNA as your next door neighbor. You were specifically created to be the YOU that he envisioned; he fashioned you with specific qualities; he designed your unique smile; structured the way you walk; crafted the way you talk; planned how you would do things differently than others; organized the way you think; decided how you would love others; and the way people would feel around you.

That uniqueness belongs to you only and no one can take it away from you. You are not a copy; you are the original blueprint that our Lord had in mind. It is impossible for you to be cloned because God has the prototype.

You ought to thank God with every fiber of your soul because you were beautifully embroidered by the master creator himself!

Be not ashamed of your genuine character, your traits were placed intentionally in you when God created you. Do not be intimidated when someone is uncomfortable around you and can't accept your uniqueness. The hard truth is, you will not be adored by everyone, you can not please everyone, and that is fine; what is imperative, however, is that you seek Jesus' approval at all times. He is the one that holds the keys of life for you, not people.

Let's remind ourselves of Psalms 139:13-14

"You made all the delicate parts of my body and knit me together in my mother's womb. Thank you for making me so distinct and wonderfully complex!
Your workmanship is marvelous — how well I know it."
(New living Translation)

Declaration:

I am uniquely created. I am not like anyone else and I am okay with that!

#Beautifully Embroidered

CHAPTER 3

You Have Great Purpose

What is your purpose? The best way to know the Lord's purpose for your life, is to fast, pray, and listen to his answer. We are each born with a divine purpose to fulfill here on earth. A unique assignment.

We are all passengers on a life journey; therefore, we need to take action in order to fulfill that purpose. The desires we have in our hearts to experience and create things, are desires that the Lord placed in our hearts when he created us. These serve as indicators of the direction he desires us to go in, and the parts of us he will use to fulfill that purpose.

Another purpose we have here on earth is to pray. We are prayer warriors, the word says we are to pray without ceasing. This is a full time job requirement that we can't ignore. Although at times you may not have the determination to pray, ask the Holy Spirit to help you, or you can start by praising God instead, this will ignite the soft fire of the Holy Spirit in you. He will then turn it into a massive prayer that can move mountains. You can start small until prayer becomes a routine in your daily life.

With this discipline, nothing can stop you from reaching your full potential. The word says you can do all things through Christ who has already given you the strength.

Philippians 4: 13, For I can do everything through Christ, Who gives me strength and He has also given you the tools to fulfill the plans for your life which will advance His Kingdom.

The jewels mentioned in Ezequiel 16:10 represent the gifts that daddy God has placed in your heart. These gifts help guide you as you pursue purpose.

In order to walk into the destiny that God has set before you, your jewels need to be used. You need to ask Him to bring forth awareness of those gifts so you can live abundantly, supernaturally, and bless others.

We have gifts that need to be resuscitated. Ask God to show you what your gifts are, so that you can implement them into your life and begin to see how glorious your life can be. Using your gifts is about fulfilling the purpose of God through you.

Declaration:

I have special gifts, strengths, passions, and talents, inside of me, that God is developing for a great purpose

#Beautifully Embroidered

CHAPTER 4

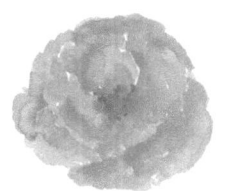

Nothing is wrong with you!

At times you might feel unimportant, destitute, unattractive, and lonely. I know there are times where you crave for acknowledgment, approval, and love from people, especially from those who are unable to return those things.

These emotions are innately sewn in us; if you are longing for man's approval, your spirit will be tarnished and continue longing for more. A longing that will never satisfy your soul. The Lord Jesus Christ, who willingly died for you on a cross, on that blazing day, is the only one who can satisfy all of your longing and needs and even surpass those needs.

Drink from that water constantly, you will never get thirsty; ask the Lord to visit you, his presence is all you need, your heart longs for Jesus.

Ergo, it is vital to dwell in his word, spent time with Holy daddy on a regular basis, sing of his name, and continue to praise him even when you have a horrible day at work. It was He that gave you that job remember?

Don't give yourself a headache, instead learn, grow, and open the doors of your heart to receive God's blessing for your life.

Lastly, it is imperative to apply the word in our daily lives so we can fully live the way God wants us to live in this world. His words satisfy our appetite. His presence fills us, mold us, humble us, and changes us forever. In Him, we can trust!

Declaration:

Only God can satisfy the longing in my soul and quench my deep thirst for love and acceptance
I trust Him.

#Beautifully Embroidered

CHAPTER 5

Your Father Loves you!

Keep reminding yourself that your daddy loves you because he genuinely does. God sacrificed his only son for YOU. You are important because God made you somebody. Beloved, You are loved with an everlasting love! Jesus bore all the pain for you on the cross; they stuck a spear into his side and His blood gushed out so that your sins would be washed away and never remembered. Isn't that love enough for you?

This is the ultimate love the world cannot offer us. God is love. Whatever negative circumstances you've experienced regarding love, He can heal you. Pray for healing; love did not fail you, people did. As you build a relationship with the Lord through His word, prayer, and church attendance, His love will heal your heart and allow you to forgive those who have hurt or betrayed you. You will feel compassion in your heart towards them rather than anger, bitterness or resentment. When you feel this shift, when the anger dissipates you will know that you have forgiven.

Forgiveness, never means that what others have done to you is okay. What it does mean, is that whatever was done to you does not have the power to impact you forever. Make a decision right now to release the negative power of unforgiveness that keeps you limited in your faith walk. Let go of all the pain, spite, strife, and Let God be the one to determine their consequences. You are more and you are bigger than what happens to you. Remember, it is the devil and his associates that work through broken people. Hurt people, hurt other people. Greater is He that dwells in YOU... Then he that is in the world. Discernment and wisdom will help you to recognize the spirits operating behind the scenes and allow you to rebuke them. John 10:10 reminds us the devil comes to kill, steal, and destroy. He does this by using compromised areas in people.

Daddy God does the complete opposite, he comes to give you life, not an ordinary life, but life in its fullest measure. Whenever you feel like you are not good enough, lovable, pretty enough, smart enough, or are feeling depressed and scared, understand the enemy is operating. God's love is reassuring, uplifting, encouraging and empowering. God's love is powerful! God's love heals. It corrects all the wrong mental messages that you have about yourself.

I pray that he renews your mind about love, heals your heart and gives you the strength to love again. Let him fill you with life, as you inhale his refreshing breath.

Declaration:

I am unconditionally loved by the father, and there is nothing that can separate me from His Everlasting Love.

#BeautifullyEmbroidered

You are Beautifully Embroidered

CHAPTER 6

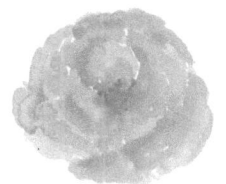

Be Constantly Aware of Whose You Are

The word says we have been made in the image of God. In Genesis 1:26 it is written: Then God said, "Let us make mankind in our image, in our likeness, so that they may rule over the fish in the sea and the birds in the sky, over the livestock and all the wild animals, and over all the creatures that move along the ground." -NIV

You are perfect just the way you are, because you resemble the Almighty. He adorned you according to His will. When you become aware of this fact, you ought to make every effort to be sanctified. Which, put simply, means to surrender your body, thoughts, soul, spirit, and mind to God and His word. Learn to lay hands on yourself and pray over yourself daily. Surrender to His will for your life. His will for your life is much different than your own will or that of other people's . When you seek Him for answers and surrender to His will, you will in turn develop sensitivity to those things that oppose His will for your life. He will lead and guide you in the path of righteousness.

When you acknowledge and believe that you are the daughter of God, you will do the necessary work to purify yourself and abstain from anything that keeps you in bondage such as alcohol, drugs, gossiping, and sexual immorality. Your soul becomes entangled and tied to the devil himself when you indulge in anything that does not glorify Christ.

The great news is that God is a redeemer, he can deliver you from this yoke; give him your life back so he can purify you, He will make you the holy place in which He resides. Ask Him for the fruit of self-control (according to Galatians 5:22), because this is his will for you.

If you have been on that path for too long, be determined to unfriend Satan; pray yourself out so God can continue to do the work that he has plan especially for you. Although it may be challenging at times decide today that you are going to live for Christ. It is the best decision you will ever make. Finding a prayer partner is a great benefit for those times when you feel like you can't prayer yourself through.

Declaration:

I am a friend of God, and will not tie my soul to Satan. Today, I walk in authority over every trick of the enemy, and walk into the fullness of a sanctified and set apart life.

#BeautifullyEmbroidered

CHAPTER 7

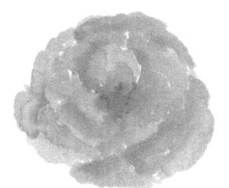

God is Perfect

The Lord is not known to make mistakes. Whatever he created is good. In Job 31:15, he responded to his friends: 'For God created both me and my servants. He created us both in the womb". We are all created beautifully in God's eye.

Whatever role we are called to play in life does not lessen our greatness. We can be great in whatever we are presently involved in. Whether it be business, house work, church, or community service. We can do all these in excellence.

When we serve in this manner, the beauty and power of who God is in us begins to shine through. Matthew 5:16 reads "Let your light so shine before men, that they may see your good works, and glorify your Father which is in heaven."

One major struggle we experience as women is learning excellence devoid of perfectionism. Although the 2 seem similar they are not. Trying to be perfect comes from the flesh, serving in excellence comes from the spirit of the Lord. You see there is no frustration in excellence, because you are aware that you are always doing the very best that you can at any given moment. In opposition, perfectionism sets unrealistic expectations that undoubtedly lead to disappointment. It's an all or nothing mentally, that leaves no room for errors and grace. We are human, life happens. Things will not always go according to plan. How we handle these mishaps stems from which place we served from.

One fail safe that will always help you differentiate is to have a mind that is set on serving others as unto the Lord. In the same manner that you would serve God, serve man. This frees you from the trap of perfectionism. Only God is perfect. Once you have set this standard for yourself, you will not have the expectations of others to be perfect either. So that you can extend grace when it is most needed.

Declaration:

I will serve my family, my job, my business, my community, my church, and my God in excellence.

#BeautifullyEmbroidered

CHAPTER 8

STOP!

As I mentioned several times in the previous chapters, being unique is a beautiful thing. It requires you to recognize that you are different because of whose you are. That you belong to the creator of the universe, and that He loves you with an everlasting love

When one is unaware of their identity in Christ, they follow the deceitful path of the world. They become a puppet in the hands of their master, which is Satan. In addition to the oppression of this world, fear comes in, low self-esteem, rejection, hopelessness, heartbroken, sickness along with everything else the devil has places in their path. This is what the word says in Leviticus 26:13 "…I broke the yoke of slavery from your neck so that you can walk with your head held high". That is to say, put on your pearls and strut through life because the Lord is by your side leading, strengthening, and protecting you. God is always with you, he will never move out of your life. His word promises us that He would never leave or forsake us.

You do not belong to this world, you are entirely for God, worshiping this world or the things in it, will never satisfy what you secretly need. The longing that your soul seeks can be found in Christ alone. Jesus is the answer, and will always remain the answer.

You are not a clown. Stop being someone that you are not! You are unique, stay genuine to that. Surrender your need for attention, approval, and to fit in. Place it all into the potter's hand; He is the one who can mold you into a perfect masterpiece. God has already removed the yoke that was placed on your neck, the oppression, the fear, the low self-esteem, the rejection and all the mistakes that you made in the past, all of it has vanished forever – once Christ died for you on the cross.

Lovely ladies, you are loved and beautifully embroidered by God. Walk into the life that God has already set for you; hang on to his hand as tight as a newborn baby holding on to his mom's fingers. Follow him with all your might, you can do it! Fear Him, honor Him, obey His principles, turn your eyes toward Jesus and receive your inheritance NOW.

Declaration:

I will allow my uniqueness to shine forth brilliantly. And place all of my needs in the hands of the Creator.

#Beautifully Embroidered

NOTES

ABOUT THE AUTHOR

Rachel Misere is a grateful daughter of the King. "Beautifully Embroidered" has been inspired by her afternoon devotionals with the Lord and is based on Ezequiel 16:10. At the request of the Lord, she started writing those beautiful words downloaded from the heart of God. Rachel seeks to glorify God through her writing and serving His people. She enjoys nature photography, fellowship, and writing.
You can find relevant articles at :
https://beautifullyembroidered.wordpress.com/

Thanks for reading! If you enjoyed it, would you kindly add a short review on Amazon and share your thoughts with me!

www.ingramcontent.com/pod-product-compliance
Lightning Source LLC
Chambersburg PA
CBHW020625300426
44113CB00007B/785